STEP-BY-STEP

MAKING BOOKS

CHARLOTTE STOWELL

ILLUSTRATED BY JIM ROBINS

Kingfisher

NEW YORK

CONTENTS

KINGFISHER
Larousse Kingfisher Chambers Inc.
95 Madison Avenue
New York, New York 10016

First American edition 1994
10 9 8 7 6 5 4 3 2 1 (HC)
10 9 8 7 6 5 4 3 2   (PB)

LIBRARY OF CONGRESS
CATALOGING-IN-PUBLICATION DATA
Robins, Deri.
Making books / by Deri Robins
and Charlotte Stowell : illustrated
by Jim Robins.—1st American ed.
p.   cm.—(Step-by-step)
1. Book design—Juvenile literature.
[1. Books.   2. Book design.
3. Handicraft.]   I. Stowell, Charlotte.
II. Robins, Jim, ill.
III. Title.   IV. Series: Step-by-step
(Kingfisher Books)
Z116.A3R6   1994
741.6'42—dc20   93-48560   CIP   AC

ISBN 1 85697 517 7 (HC)
ISBN 1 85697 518 5 (PB)

Edited by Deri Robins
Designed by Ben White
Illustrations by Jim Robins
Photographed by Rolf Cornell,
 SCL Photographic Services
Cover design by Terry Woodley
Typeset in 3B2 by
 Tracey McNerney
Printed in Hong Kong

WHAT YOU NEED

First of all, you'll need to get together a basic bookmaker's kit like the one shown in the photo. You'll also need a thick piece of cardboard or masonite to protect your work surface from paint, cuts, and scratches.

Paper and Cardboard

You'll need plenty of thick paper or thin cardboard to make pages, and heavier board for hard covers.

Practice making books from scrap paper first. Then visit an art store to see the huge choice of paper and board available!

Glue

White glue or paste is good for sticking paper and cardboard together, and for making collages.

For more heavy-duty gluing (attaching a cover, for example), use safe household glues— *not* superglue.

Stapler

Bias tape

Glue

Craft knife

Scissors

Metal ruler

White glue

Ribbon

Tools of the Trade

To sew the pages of your books, you'll need a big darning needle, some strong thread, and a pair of scissors. A stapler can also be used to make some simple books.

You'll need a craft knife and a metal ruler to cut the cardboard and paper. *Always* make sure an adult is around to watch and help when you're doing any cutting.

Other Things

Among the other things you'll need are: poster paints, felt-tip pens, and colored pencils for coloring your books; strips of strong tape or bias binding for making hard covers; scraps of ribbon; colored fabric and paper; and a few large spring clips.

Poster paints

Strong thread

Paper and cardboard

Spring clip

Felt-tip pens

Pencils

Cotton binding

Brushes

String

MAKING BOOKS

The following pages show you how to make books of all shapes and sizes—just follow the step-by-step instructions carefully. Here are some tips on cutting and folding, along with some of the terms you'll meet throughout the book.

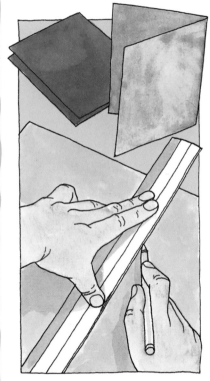

The *illustrations* are the pictures in your book.

A *spread* is two pages that face each other.

The *text* is all the words in the book.

The *heading* is usually bigger than the other words on the page.

STEGOSAURU

Folding

Folding cardboard and thick paper is easier if you run a used-up ballpoint (or the back of your craft knife) lightly over the line first—this is called *scoring*.

Endpapers are stuck between the covers and the first and last pages of the book.

Spine

Front cover

Although the books shown on the following pages come in many different shapes and sizes, the basic parts are the same. These parts are labeled here.

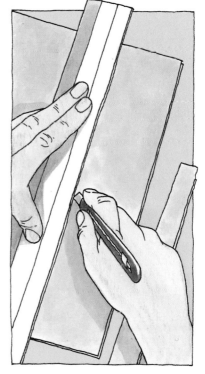

Cutting

Craft knives are very sharp and need to be handled with care!

Don't press too hard—several light strokes are best. A metal ruler will help you to keep the lines straight.

The *gutter* runs down the middle of the spread.

FOLDERS AND WALLETS

Folders and wallets have lots of different uses—unlike real books, you can change the contents as often as you like! You can also tuck in extra bits and pieces, such as maps, photos, magazine clippings—even a booklet or two.

Folder

Fold a big piece of fairly stiff cardboard in half (see the notes on folding and scoring on page 6).

Cut another piece slightly smaller than one half of the folder, and with flaps on two sides.

Cut several more pieces of cardboard, each smaller than the last. Fold the flaps and glue them inside the folder as shown. Leave to dry.

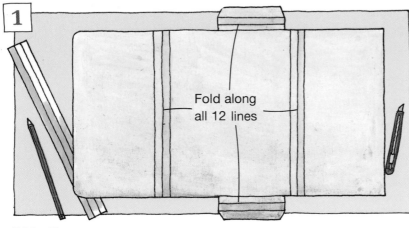

1 Fold along all 12 lines

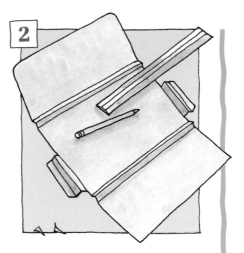

2

Wallet

With a pencil and a ruler, copy the pattern shown above onto a sheet of thick paper or thin cardboard.

Cut it out, using a ruler and a craft knife. Score all the inside lines with an old ballpoint, or the back of the craft knife.

Fold along the lines. Make the middle fold first, then fold in the opposite direction along the two other folds.

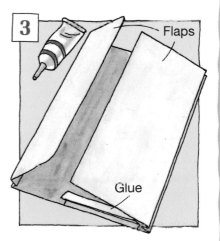

3 Flaps

Glue

To finish your wallet, glue the top of the side flaps inside the bottom fold, as shown.

Left: A colorful selection of wallets and folders made from cardboard.

SEWING THE PAGES

The following pages show three different ways of sewing the pages of your book.

If you want to add a cover (see pages 14-15) to the books shown in methods A and B, you must strengthen the spine with a strip of cardboard. However, if you don't want a hard cover, you can leave this out.

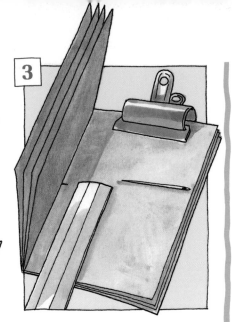

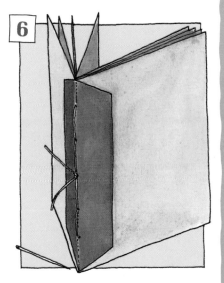

Strip of card to strengthen spine

Method A

Take up to six pieces of heavy paper or thin cardboard. Fold them in the middle, and stack them inside each other to make a book.

Cut a strip of cardboard the same length as your book. Trim the top and bottom diagonally, as shown, and fold around the spine of your book.

Hold the pages of your book tightly in place with a spring clip. Then mark the middle point along the gutter with a ruler and pencil.

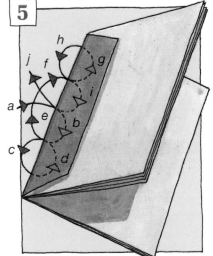

Add two more marks on each side of the middle mark, making them the same distance apart. Make a hole through the pencil marks with a darning needle.

Push the needle and thread through the middle mark, starting from the outside. Keep sewing in and out, following the direction shown above.

You should end up with two loose ends of thread outside the spine, as here. Tie them together with a double knot in the middle, and trim the ends with scissors.

11

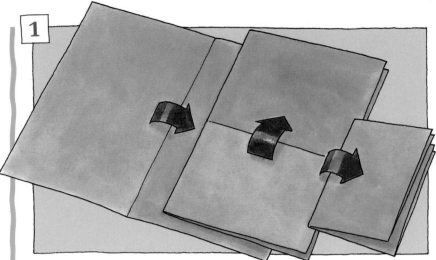

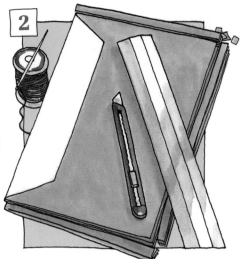

Method B

Fold a big piece of paper in half several times (two folds make an 8-page book, three folds make a 16-page book, and four folds make 32 pages). Add a strip of cardboard along the spine as shown in step 2 of method A (see page 11).

Sew exactly as shown for method A. With a ruler and craft knife, neatly trim all the edges except the spine.

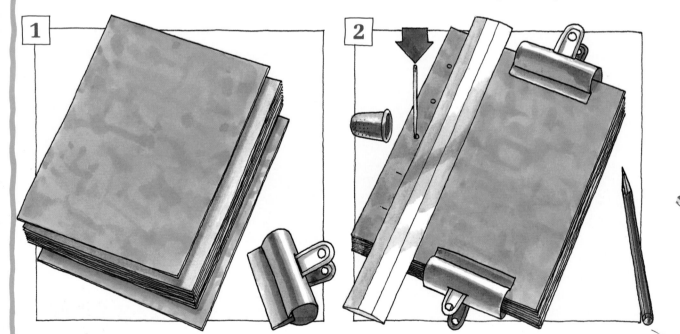

Method C

Take several sheets of paper of the same size, and stack them in a pile. Cut two cardboard covers and place them at the top and bottom of the pile. Hold everything in place with spring clips.

With a ruler and pencil, draw a line $\frac{1}{4}$ inch in from the spine. Mark five points along the line, all the same distance apart, and pierce them with a darning needle.

3

Thread the needle with strong thread. Sew around the spine in the direction shown in the picture.

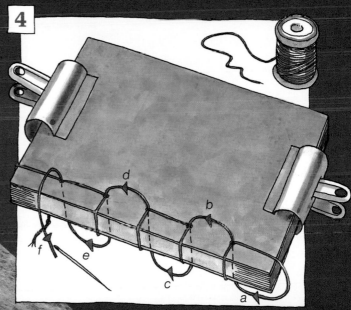

4

Then sew back along the spine in the opposite direction. Tie the two loose ends together.

MAKING COVERS

The simplest kind of cover to make is a soft cardboard wrapper. However, if you want the book to be really strong and long-lasting, you could try gluing the pages into a hard cover, with a spine made from cotton binding or bias tape.

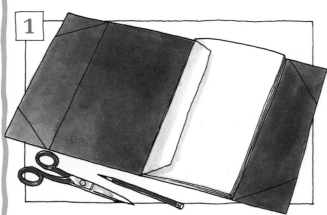

Wrapper Cover

Measure and cut out a piece of thick paper the same height as the pages of your book, but twice as wide, and with a wide flap at each end.

Trim the wrapper flaps top and bottom, then score and fold them in. Fold the wrapper in half, and lay the book inside.

Cut a flap in the middle of the front and back pages. Fold and tuck in the cover flaps, as shown.

1

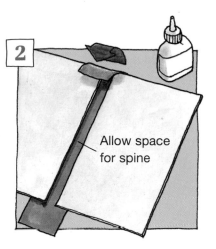

2

Allow space for spine

3

Hard Cover

Cut out two pieces of strong cardboard. Make them about $^3/_{16}$ inch wider than the pages of your book on all sides.

Glue the pieces onto a strip of cloth, allowing an extra $1^1/_2$ inches at the top and bottom. Fold the extra pieces over and glue.

Cut two pieces of paper, 2 inches wider than the boards on the top, outer, and bottom edges. Trim the corners of the papers and glue to the boards as shown.

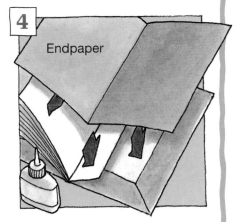

4

Endpaper

Glue the back of the piece of strengthening board to the cover. Then glue the first and last pages of the book to the inside of the covers. Or, cut two separate endpapers from colored paper and glue them between the cover and the book.

PRINTING PATTERNS

Try printing designs onto your covers—use poster paints for the stencils and printing blocks, and oil paints for marbling.

You can also make beautiful patterned endpapers in the same way, or even print directly onto the pages of your book.

Stenciling

Draw a design on stenciling board or ordinary thin cardboard. Carefully cut out the holes with a craft knife.

Hold the board down on the cover and dab thick poster paint over the holes with a piece of sponge or a stenciling brush.

Printing Blocks

Cut some shapes out of foam rubber and glue them to thick squares of wood or cardboard.

Dip the shapes into thick paint and press them down to print. When the paint is dry, you could add some extra details by using a darker color.

Marbling

Half-fill a wide tray with water. Mix some oil paint with mineral spirits until runny, then dribble them across the water.

Swirl the water gently with a clean brush, then lay a sheet of paper on top.

Smooth carefully, lift off, and leave to dry.

COLLAGE COVERS

Magazines, newspapers, and greeting cards can all be cut up and glued to your covers to make a collage. You can also use bits of junk to make pictures and patterns—they look best if you paint them afterward. A coat of clear varnish will stop the paint from rubbing off the covers.

Collage Castle

This castle was made from tree bark, aluminum foil, sandpaper, toothpicks, pencils, and bamboo—but you could use all kinds of spare junk! The moon was made from half a cashew nut.

Once the glue was dry, the castle was painted silver-gray.

Découpage

Cut pictures out of old wrapping paper, magazines, or news-papers, and glue them to your cover to make an overlapping pattern.

Look for interesting colors, pictures, and shades. Try tearing some of the pages—this gives a softer edge than cutting them.

Antique Book

Cut out some shapes from cardboard and some short lengths of string. Glue them to the cover in a pattern.

Brush black paint along the raised edges, then leave to dry. Rub gold paint over the cover with a dry brush.

BOOKMARKS

Make bookmarks from leftover cardboard! If your book has a theme, your bookmark could match it— for example, a monster bookmark could hang over the pages of a scary story!

1

Draw and cut a bookmark out of cardboard. Paint it, or decorate it by gluing on some cardboard shapes. Draw a flap and cut it out with a craft knife.

2

Slot the flap over a page in your book. You could also make a flap by gluing on an extra piece of cardboard (like the parrot's wing, see right)—only the top should be glued to the bookmark.

A Book Ribbon

Tuck a piece of ribbon between the piece of strengthening cardboard and the cloth spine before you glue them together—the ribbon should be about 2 inches longer than the length of the book.

These bookmarks come in all shapes and sizes—some hang over the pages by their paws, others by their tails, flippers, or wings!

DESIGNING BOOKS

Now that you've made your book, what are you going to do with it? You may want to use the book as a diary or a notebook, or to give it to someone as a gift. On the other hand, you could use it to write and illustrate a story, a poem, or anything else at all. Here's how you go about it.

Count how many pages you have in your book, then draw them on a piece of paper. This is called a *page plan*. It will help you to work out where you want your text and illustrations to go.

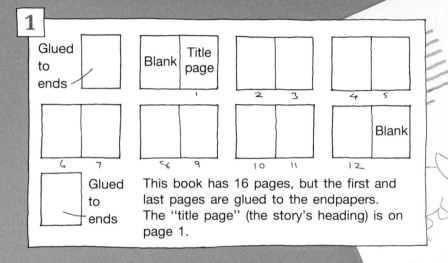

This book has 16 pages, but the first and last pages are glued to the endpapers. The "title page" (the story's heading) is on page 1.

Decide how many lines of text to put on each page. Some pages can have more text than others, as you can see from the designs shown here.

22

3

Plan where your text and illustrations will go.

4

Draw a writing guide on cardboard (the same size as a page from your book). Use a black pen, and keep the spaces between the lines equal.

Vary the position of the text and pictures—some ideas are shown here.

5

Write the words and pictures lightly in your book in pencil. Slip the writing guide under the page to help keep the lines of text even.

ADDING PICTURES

When you're happy with the way your designs look, you can use your pens and paints to fill in the words and pictures.

Do the illustrations first, using some of the suggestions on these pages. Then carefully write the words around the pictures.

The dinosaur spreads below were painted, while the planets and rockets were made by gluing on pieces of cardboard and paper.

The spread on the far right shows how magazines can be cut up and arranged to make collage pictures.

Painting

You can draw or paint the illustrations directly onto the pages. Or trace some pictures from your favorite books and magazines and color them in.

Paper Shapes

Cut shapes from cardboard or paper and glue them to the pages to make pictures (most of the photos in this book show books illustrated in this way).

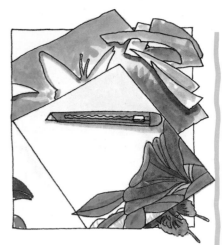

Collage

Cut pictures from old color magazines and glue them into your book.

You could also use newspapers, photos you've taken yourself, or photocopies.

NOVELTY NOTEBOOKS

Notebooks can be quickly sewn or stapled to make presents for birthdays or Christmas—they can be any shape or size, as long as you remember to leave most of the folded edge uncut. You can either leave the insides blank, or write in special messages or information.

1 Fold several sheets of thick paper together. Draw on the design for your book, and sew down the middle of the pages (see page 11).

2 Cut around the outline of the notebook as shown. Make sure you don't cut any of the thread that holds the spine of the book together.

Paint the front, or use some of the printing ideas on page 17. You could also glue on loops of cardboard to hold a pen or pencil.

Instead of sewing the books, you could staple along the spine—as we did to make the birthday cake book.

The snowman, elephant, and sunflower are all sewn. The birthday cake book is stapled down the side.

To make the butterfly, cut several wing-shaped pages and sew down the middle. Cut out the body separately, and glue it over the stitches.

ZIGZAG BOOKS

Zigzag books don't need any sewing! They can be written and read just like ordinary books, or unfolded and pinned to the wall to make a frieze.

These books look best if you make them out of heavy paper or thin cardboard.

Simple Zigzag

1

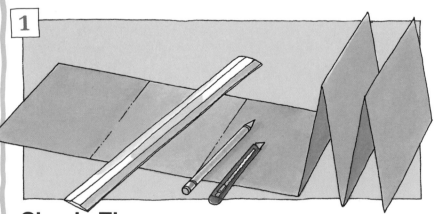

Divide a long strip of thin cardboard or thick paper into equal parts using a ruler and a pencil.

Fold the paper into a zigzag. Then add your illustrations and text (if any).

2

Decorate both sides—use them to make long, foldout friezes or to tell a story.

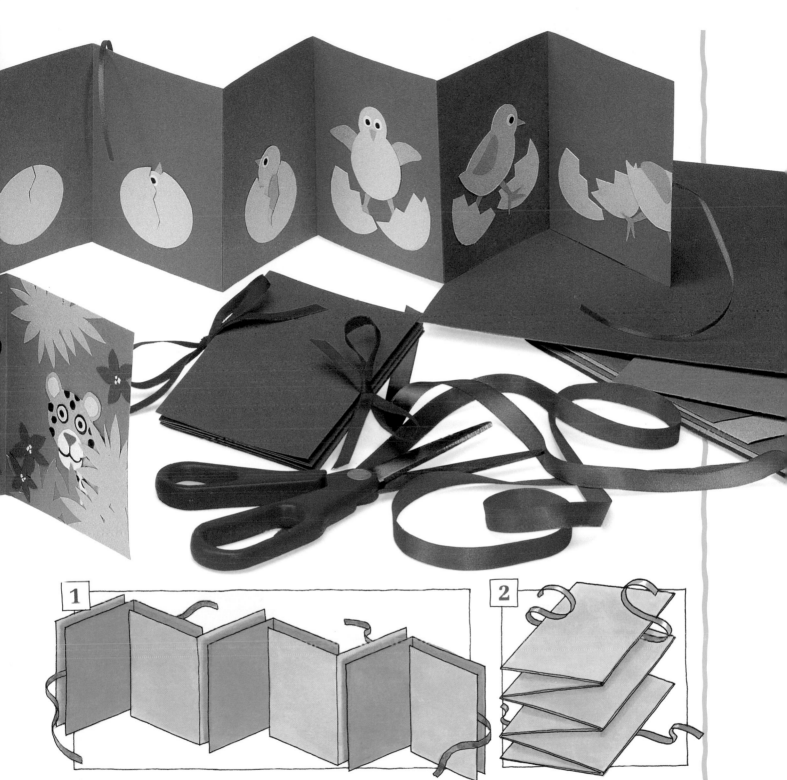

Two-color Zigzag

Take three sheets of paper in one color and three in another color. Fold them in half, and cut one of the pieces in two. Glue together to make a zigzag, with the two cut pieces at each end.

You could glue ribbon under the end pieces to tie up the zigzag, as shown.

POP-UP BOOKS

How about having pop-up pictures in your books? They look very impressive, but aren't that difficult to make. Like the flaps and moving parts on pages 33-36, pop-ups work best in books with fewer than ten pages made of thin cardboard.

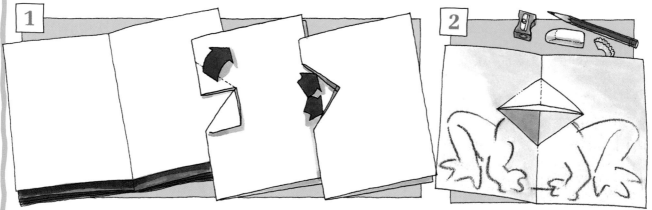

Mouths and Beaks

Cut a piece of cardboard the same size as a spread in your book. Fold the paper, and cut a slit near the middle. Fold back the flaps, and tuck in.

When you open the page, the flaps will open like a mouth or beak!

Color the picture, then glue the page into your book. Don't put any glue on the back of the mouth or beak.

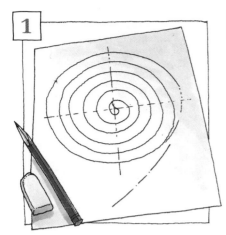

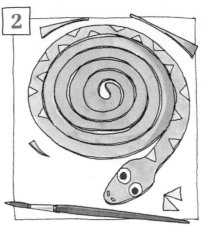

Spirals

Draw a circle on some thin cardboard, slightly smaller than a page from your book. Draw a spiral inside the circle.

Draw a snake's head at the outer edge of the circle, as shown. Cut around all the lines with scissors.

Use paints, felt-tip pens, or bits of colored paper to decorate the snake and to make a colorful jungle background.

Glue the *back* of the snake's head to the right-hand page. Put a dab of glue on the *top* of its tail. Shut the book, press together, then open and leave to dry.

You can glue on extra details made from cardboard, such as this frog's bulging eyes!

31

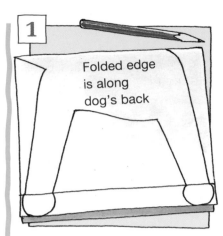

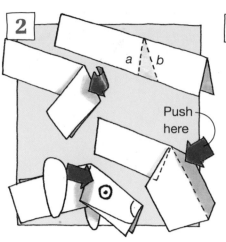

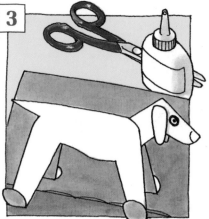

Stand-up Dog

Fold a 3 x 5½-inch piece of cardboard in half. Draw the shape of the dog's body and cut it out so that the folded edge is along the dog's back.

Fold a 1½ x 3½-inch piece of cardboard in half. Make folds *a* and *b*. Open and push down to make the head. Cut and glue on the ears.

Fold back the paws on the other side. Dab the undersides with glue, and fold the facing page on top of them.

Glue the neck into the body. Fold the paws back on one side, and glue the undersides to one of the pages, ½ inch from the gutter.

You can decorate your stand-up animals before gluing them into your book. This dog's spots were made with a hole-puncher and then glued to the body.

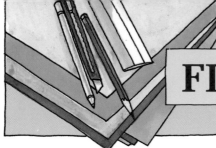

FLAPS AND MOVERS

You can add even more fun and excitement to your books by making flaps that open, holes to peek through, and wheels that turn! You could also use these methods to make really special greeting cards.

Flaps

Simple doors and windows can be glued straight into your book.

You can also cut flaps from a separate page of cardboard, and glue the page into the book.

Peepholes

Peepholes such as keyholes and window panes can be cut from the cover or inside pages to show part of the picture on the page underneath.

Mix and Match

Cut a small book into three sections. Draw a figure on the front. Open the flaps, and mark where the neck and legs join. Draw a new figure on each page.

Wheels

Cut out a cardboard wheel ³/₈-inch smaller than a page in your book.

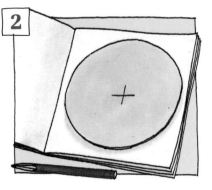

Put the wheel on the page, and draw around it. Mark both centers.

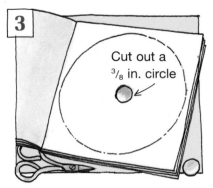

Cut out a ³/₈ in. circle

Measure a ³/₈-inch circle around the mark on the page and cut it out.

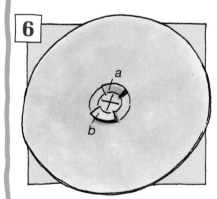

Semicircle

Cut a semicircle from the page edge, and also from the page beneath it.

Window ³/₈ in.

Cut out a window, leaving ³/₈ inch between the outer edge of the

circle and the window, and ³/₈-inch between the window and the center.

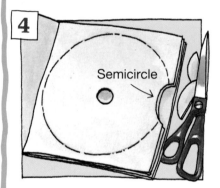

a

b

Draw a ³/₄-inch circle in the middle of the wheel, with a ³/₈-inch circle inside it. Cut and fold up flaps *a* and *b* as shown.

Fold flaps back

Lay the wheel under the page, and push the flaps through the hole. Turn the wheel around, and draw inside the window.

Glue the edges of the page to the one underneath. Then glue another small circle to the flaps— *not* to the page.

Your wheel could show ghosts in a haunted castle . . . or a changing view from a porthole!

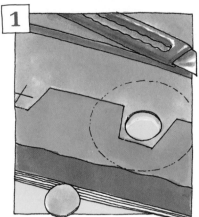

1

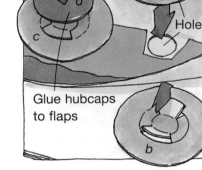

2

Hole

Glue hubcaps
to flaps

a

c
d

b

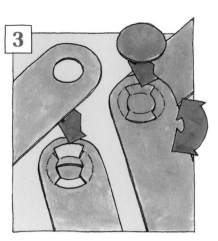

3

Moving Machines

Draw a machine onto a
page in your book, or
make the picture from
shapes cut from
cardboard. Draw the
outline of a wheel, and
cut a $\frac{3}{8}$-inch circle from
the middle of the wheel.

Cut two cardboard
wheels, one with flaps
(see page 34), and one
with a $\frac{3}{8}$-inch hole in the
center. Assemble as
shown. Cut a hubcap from
cardboard, and glue it
onto the flaps.

You can join other
moving parts in the same
way. Just cut a hole in
one of the parts, and
flaps in the other. Slot
together as shown, and
cover with circles cut
from cardboard.

PEEK-IN BOOKS

Here's a very special bookmaking project, and once again, it's much simpler than it looks! The book has five spreads, so if you want to use it for a story or a poem, you'll have to divide your text into five separate sections.

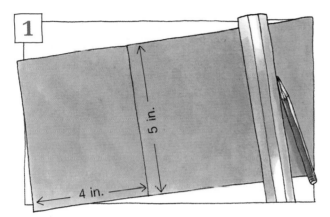

1

To make the background for the book, cut a strip of thin cardboard 5 x 40 inches. Use a ruler to divide it into ten pages, each 4 inches wide.

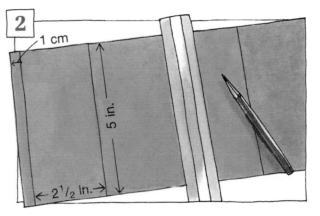

2

Cut a strip measuring 5 x 25 inches for the foreground. Allow a ¹/₂-inch flap at each end. Divide the rest of the strip into ten pages, each 2¹/₂ inches wide .

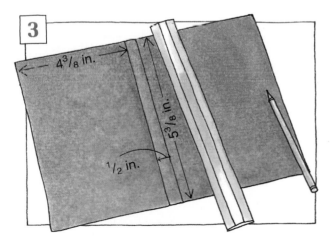

3

Cut a slightly thicker piece of cardboard for the cover (5³/₈ x 9¹/₄ inches). Measure a spine ¹/₂ inch wide down the middle and score along the lines.

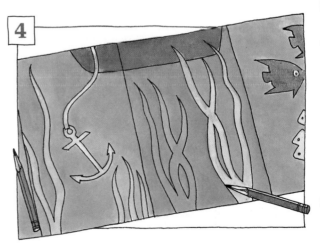

4

Draw and color the five background spreads (each spread is made up of two pages). It's best to keep these pictures quite simple.

You can use paint to decorate the foreground and background, or glue shapes cut from cardboard, as shown here.

5

Plan illustrations for the five foreground spreads, allowing for peepholes in each one. Paint the spreads, or glue on cutout pictures.

6

Fold both the strips carefully into zig-zags, as shown above. Fold the two $\frac{1}{2}$-inch flaps at both ends of the foreground strip outward.

7 Put short lengths of ribbon between the cover and the first and last pages of the background strip, then glue the pages to the cover.

8 Put a thin line of glue down all the folded edges of the background strip and on the flaps of the foreground. Glue the two strips together.

Several books can be put into
a box called a *slipcase*. Cut the
case shape shown from cardboard, using
the size of the books as a guide.

The length and width of the case
should be about $1/2$ inch longer than the
books, and the depth should be $1/2$ inch
wider than the spines of the books when
they're stacked together. Add flaps, fold
up, and glue into a case.

Length

Width

Depth

Flaps

Slipcase

Scroll

Fridge
magnet
notebook

Scrolls were among
the earliest types of book.
Make one by rolling up a sheet
of paper and tying with ribbon—
add a "seal" cut from cardboard,
if you like.

Try gluing a magnet to the back of a
tiny book, and sticking it on the fridge!